# The Masque of Pandora by Henry Wadsworth Longfellow

Henry Wadsworth Longfellow was born on February 27th, 1807 in Portland, Maine. As a young boy, it was obvious that he was very studious and he quickly became fluent in Latin.

He published his first poem, "The Battle of Lovell's Pond", in the Portland Gazette on November 17th, 1820. He was already thinking of a career in literature and, in his senior year, wrote to his father: "I will not disguise it in the least... the fact is, I most eagerly aspire after future eminence in literature, my whole soul burns most ardently after it, and every earthly thought centers in it...."

After graduation travels in Europe occupied the next three years and he seemed to easily absorb any language he set himself to learn.

On September 14th, 1831, Longfellow married Mary Storer Potter. They settled in Brunswick.

His first published book was in 1833, a translation of poems by the Spanish poet Jorge Manrique. He also published a travel book, Outre-Mer: A Pilgrimage Beyond the Sea.

During a trip to Europe Mary became pregnant. Sadly, in October 1835, she miscarried at some six months. After weeks of illness she died, at the age of 22 on November 29th, 1835. Longfellow wrote "One thought occupies me night and day... She is dead — She is dead! All day I am weary and sad".

In late 1839, Longfellow published Hyperion, a book in prose inspired by his trips abroad.

Ballads and Other Poems was published in 1841 and included "The Village Blacksmith" and "The Wreck of the Hesperus". His reputation as a poet, and a commercial one at that, was set.

On May 10th, 1843, after seven years in pursuit of a chance for new love, Longfellow received word from Fanny Appleton that she agreed to marry him.

On November 1st, 1847, the epic poem Evangeline was published.

In 1854, Longfellow retired from Harvard, to devote himself entirely to writing.

The Song of Haiwatha, perhaps his best known and enjoyed work was published in 1855.

On July 10th, 1861, after suffering horrific burns the previous day. In his attempts to save her Longfellow had also been badly burned and was unable to attend her funeral.

He spent several years translating Dante Alighieri's Divine Comedy. It was published in 1867.

Longfellow was also part of a group who became known as The Fireside Poets which also included William Cullen Bryant, John Greenleaf Whittier, James Russell Lowell, and Oliver Wendell Holmes Snr.

Longfellow was the most popular poet of his day. As a friend once wrote to him, "no other poet was so fully recognized in his lifetime". Some of his works including "Paul Revere's Ride" and "The Song of Haiwatha" may have rewritten the facts but became essential parts of the American psyche and culture.

Henry Wadsworth Longfellow died, surrounded by family, on Friday, March 24th, 1882. He had been suffering from peritonitis.

## Index of Contents

THE MASQUE OF PANDORA

I

THE WORKSHOP OF HEPHAESTUS

**HEPHAESTUS** [Standing before the statue of Pandora]
Not fashioned out of gold, like Hera's throne,
Nor forged of iron like the thunderbolts
Of Zeus omnipotent, or other works
Wrought by my hands at Lemnos or Olympus,
But moulded in soft clay, that unresisting
Yields itself to the touch, this lovely form
Before me stands, perfect in every part.
Not Aphrodite's self appeared more fair,
When first upwafted by caressing winds
She came to high Olympus, and the gods
Paid homage to her beauty.  Thus her hair
Was cinctured; thus her floating drapery
Was like a cloud about her, and her face
Was radiant with the sunshine and the sea.

**THE VOICE OF ZEUS**
Is thy work done, Hephaestus?

**HEPHAESTUS**
It is finished!

**THE VOICE**
Not finished till I breathe the breath of life
Into her nostrils, and she moves and speaks.

**HEPHAESTUS**
Will she become immortal like ourselves?

**THE VOICE**
The form that thou hast fashioned out of clay
Is of the earth and mortal; but the spirit,
The life, the exhalation of my breath,
Is of diviner essence and immortal.
The gods shall shower on her their benefactions,
She shall possess all gifts: the gift of song,
The gift of eloquence, the gift of beauty,
The fascination and the nameless charm
That shall lead all men captive.

**HEPHAESTUS**
Wherefore? wherefore?

(A wind shakes the house.)

I hear the rushing of a mighty wind
Through all the halls and chambers of my house!
Her parted lips inhale it, and her bosom
Heaves with the inspiration. As a reed
Beside a river in the rippling current
Bends to and fro, she bows or lifts her head.
She gazes round about as if amazed;
She is alive; she breathes, but yet she speaks not!

[**PANDORA** descends from the pedestal.]


CHORUS OF THE GRACES

**AGLAIA**
In the workshop of Hephaestus
What is this I see?
Have the Gods to four increased us
Who were only three?
Beautiful in form and feature,
Lovely as the day,
Can there be so fair a creature
Formed of common clay?

**THALIA**

O sweet, pale face! O lovely eyes of azure,
Clear as the waters of a brook that run
Limpid and laughing in the summer sun!
O golden hair that like a miser's treasure
In its abundance overflows the measure!
O graceful form, that cloudlike floatest on
With the soft, undulating gait of one
Who moveth as if motion were a pleasure!
By what name shall I call thee? Nymph or Muse,
Callirrhoe or Urania? Some sweet name
Whose every syllable is a caress
Would best befit thee; but I cannot choose,
Nor do I care to choose; for still the same,
Nameless or named, will be thy loveliness.

**EUPHROSYNE**

Dowered with all celestial gifts,
Skilled in every art
That ennobles and uplifts
And delights the heart,
Fair on earth shall be thy fame
As thy face is fair,
And Pandora be the name
Thou henceforth shalt bear.


II

OLYMPUS

**HERMES** [Pputting on his sandals.]
Much must he toil who serves the Immortal Gods,
And I, who am their herald, most of all.
No rest have I, nor respite. I no sooner
Unclasp the winged sandals from my feet,
Than I again must clasp them, and depart
Upon some foolish errand. But to-day
The errand is not foolish. Never yet
With greater joy did I obey the summons
That sends me earthward. I will fly so swiftly
That my caduceus in the whistling air
Shall make a sound like the Pandaean pipes,
Cheating the shepherds; for to-day I go,
Commissioned by high-thundering Zeus, to lead
A maiden to Prometheus, in his tower,
And by my cunning arguments persuade him

To marry her.  What mischief lies concealed
In this design I know not; but I know
Who thinks of marrying hath already taken
One step upon the road to penitence.
Such embassies delight me.  Forth I launch
On the sustaining air, nor fear to fall
Like Icarus, nor swerve aside like him
Who drove amiss Hyperion's fiery steeds.
I sink, I fly! The yielding element
Folds itself round about me like an arm,
And holds me as a mother holds her child.


III

TOWER OF PROMETHEUS ON MOUNT CAUCASUS

**PROMETHEUS**
I hear the trumpet of Alectryon
Proclaim the dawn.  The stars begin to fade,
And all the heavens are full of prophecies
And evil auguries.  Blood-red last night
I saw great Kronos rise; the crescent moon
Sank through the mist, as if it were the scythe
His parricidal hand had flung far down
The western steeps.  O ye Immortal Gods,
What evil are ye plotting and contriving?

[**HERMES** and **PANDORA** at the threshold.]

**PANDORA**
I cannot cross the threshold.  An unseen
And icy hand repels me.  These blank walls
Oppress me with their weight!

**PROMETHEUS**
Powerful ye are,
But not omnipotent.  Ye cannot fight
Against Necessity.  The Fates control you,
As they do us, and so far we are equals!

**PANDORA**
Motionless, passionless, companionless,
He sits there muttering in his beard.  His voice
Is like a river flowing underground!

**HERMES**

Prometheus, hail!

**PROMETHEUS**
Who calls me?

**HERMES**
It is I.
Dost thou not know me?

**PROMETHEUS**
By thy winged cap
And winged heels I know thee.  Thou art Hermes,
Captain of thieves!  Hast thou again been stealing
The heifers of Admetus in the sweet
Meadows of asphodel? or Hera's girdle?
Or the earth-shaking trident of Poseidon?

**HERMES**
And thou, Prometheus; say, hast thou again
Been stealing fire from Helios' chariot-wheels
To light thy furnaces?

**PROMETHEUS**
Why comest thou hither
So early in the dawn?

**HERMES**
The Immortal Gods
Know naught of late or early.  Zeus himself
The omnipotent hath sent me.

**PROMETHEUS**
For what purpose?

**HERMES**
To bring this maiden to thee.

**PROMETHEUS**
I mistrust
The Gods and all their gifts. If they have sent her
It is for no good purpose.

**HERMES**
What disaster
Could she bring on thy house, who is a woman?

**PROMETHEUS**
The Gods are not my friends, nor am I theirs.

Whatever comes from them, though in a shape
As beautiful as this, is evil only.
Who art thou?

**PANDORA**
One who, though to thee unknown,
Yet knoweth thee.

**PROMETHEUS**
How shouldst thou know me, woman?

**PANDORA**
Who knoweth not Prometheus the humane?

**PROMETHEUS**
Prometheus the unfortunate; to whom
Both Gods and men have shown themselves ungrateful.
When every spark was quenched on every hearth
Throughout the earth, I brought to man the fire
And all its ministrations. My reward
Hath been the rock and vulture.

**HERMES**
But the Gods
At last relent and pardon.

**PROMETHEUS**
They relent not;
They pardon not; they are implacable,
Revengeful, unforgiving!

**HERMES**
As a pledge
Of reconciliation they have sent to thee
This divine being, to be thy companion,
And bring into thy melancholy house
The sunshine and the fragrance of her youth.

**PROMETHEUS**
I need them not. I have within myself
All that my heart desires; the ideal beauty
Which the creative faculty of mind
Fashions and follows in a thousand shapes
More lovely than the real. My own thoughts
Are my companions; my designs and labors
And aspirations are my only friends.

**HERMES**

Decide not rashly. The decision made
Can never be recalled. The Gods implore not,
Plead not, solicit not; they only offer
Choice and occasion, which once being passed
Return no more. Dost thou accept the gift?

**PROMETHEUS**

No gift of theirs, in whatsoever shape
It comes to me, with whatsoever charm
To fascinate my sense, will I receive.
Leave me.

**PANDORA**

Let us go hence. I will not stay.

**HERMES**

We leave thee to thy vacant dreams, and all
The silence and the solitude of thought,
The endless bitterness of unbelief,
The loneliness of existence without love.

CHORUS OF THE FATES

**CLOTHO**

How the Titan, the defiant,
The self-centred, self-reliant,
Wrapped in visions and illusions,
Robs himself of life's best gifts!
Till by all the storm-winds shaken,
By the blast of fate o'ertaken,
Hopeless, helpless, and forsaken,
In the mists of his confusions
To the reefs of doom he drifts!

**LACHESIS**

Sorely tried and sorely tempted,
From no agonies exempted,
In the penance of his trial,
And the discipline of pain;
Often by illusions cheated,
Often baffled and defeated
In the tasks to be completed,
He, by toil and self-denial,
To the highest shall attain.

**ATROPOS**

Tempt no more the noble schemer;
Bear unto some idle dreamer
This new toy and fascination,
This new dalliance and delight!
To the garden where reposes
Epimetheus crowned with roses,
To the door that never closes
Upon pleasure and temptation,
Bring this vision of the night!


IV

THE AIR

**HERMES** [Returning to Olympus.]
As lonely as the tower that he inhabits,
As firm and cold as are the crags about him,
Prometheus stands.  The thunderbolts of Zeus
Alone can move him; but the tender heart
Of Epimetheus, burning at white heat,
Hammers and flames like all his brother's forges!
Now as an arrow from Hyperion's bow,
My errand done, I fly, I float, I soar
Into the air, returning to Olympus.
O joy of motion!  O delight to cleave
The infinite realms of space, the liquid ether,
Through the warm sunshine and the cooling cloud,
Myself as light as sunbeam or as cloud!
With one touch of my swift and winged feet,
I spurn the solid earth, and leave it rocking
As rocks the bough from which a bird takes wing.


V

THE HOUSE OF EPIMETHEUS

**EPIMETHEUS**
Beautiful apparition! go not hence!
Surely thou art a Goddess, for thy voice
Is a celestial melody, and thy form
Self-poised as if it floated on the air!

**PANDORA**
No Goddess am I, nor of heavenly birth,

But a mere woman fashioned out of clay
And mortal as the rest.

**EPIMETHEUS**
Thy face is fair;
There is a wonder in thine azure eyes
That fascinates me. Thy whole presence seems
A soft desire, a breathing thought of love.
Say, would thy star like Merope's grow dim
If thou shouldst wed beneath thee?

**PANDORA**
Ask me not;
I cannot answer thee. I only know
The Gods have sent me hither.

**EPIMETHEUS**
I believe,
And thus believing am most fortunate.
It was not Hermes led thee here, but Eros,
And swifter than his arrows were thine eyes
In wounding me. There was no moment's space
Between my seeing thee and loving thee.
O, what a telltale face thou hast! Again
I see the wonder in thy tender eyes.

**PANDORA**
They do but answer to the love in thine,
Yet secretly I wonder thou shouldst love me.
Thou knowest me not.

**EPIMETHEUS**
Perhaps I know thee better
Than had I known thee longer. Yet it seems
That I have always known thee, and but now
Have found thee. Ah, I have been waiting long.

**PANDORA**
How beautiful is this house! The atmosphere
Breathes rest and comfort, and the many chambers
Seem full of welcomes.

**EPIMETHEUS**
They not only seem,
But truly are. This dwelling and its master
Belong to thee.

**PANDORA**

Here let me stay forever!
There is a spell upon me.

**EPIMETHEUS**
Thou thyself
Art the enchantress, and I feel thy power
Envelop me, and wrap my soul and sense
In an Elysian dream.

**PANDORA**
O, let me stay.
How beautiful are all things round about me,
Multiplied by the mirrors on the walls!
What treasures hast thou here! Yon oaken chest,
Carven with figures and embossed with gold,
Is wonderful to look upon! What choice
And precious things dost thou keep hidden in it?

**EPIMETHEUS**
I know not. 'T is a mystery.

**PANDORA**
Hast thou never
Lifted the lid?

**EPIMETHEUS**
The oracle forbids.
Safely concealed there from all mortal eyes
Forever sleeps the secret of the Gods.
Seek not to know what they have hidden from thee,
Till they themselves reveal it.

**PANDORA**
As thou wilt.

**EPIMETHEUS**
Let us go forth from this mysterious place.
The garden walks are pleasant at this hour;
The nightingales among the sheltering boughs
Of populous and many-nested trees
Shall teach me how to woo thee, and shall tell me
By what resistless charms or incantations
They won their mates.

**PANDORA**
Thou dost not need a teacher.

(They go out.)

CHORUS OF THE EUMENIDES

What the Immortals
Confide to thy keeping,
Tell unto no man;
Waking or sleeping,
Closed be thy portals
To friend as to foeman.

Silence conceals it;
The word that is spoken
Betrays and reveals it;
By breath or by token
The charm may be broken.

With shafts of their splendors
The Gods unforgiving
Pursue the offenders,
The dead and the living!
Fortune forsakes them,
Nor earth shall abide them,
Nor Tartarus hide them;
Swift wrath overtakes them!

With useless endeavor,
Forever, forever,
Is Sisyphus rolling
His stone up the mountain!
Immersed in the fountain,
Tantalus tastes not
The water that wastes not!
Through ages increasing
The pangs that afflict him,
With motion unceasing
The wheel of Ixion
Shall torture its victim!

VI

IN THE GARDEN

**EPIMETHEUS**

Yon snow-white cloud that sails sublime in ether
Is but the sovereign Zeus, who like a swan

Flies to fair-ankled Leda!

**PANDORA**
Or perchance
Ixion's cloud, the shadowy shape of Hera,
That bore the Centaurs.

**EPIMETHEUS**
The divine and human.

**CHORUS OF BIRDS**
Gently swaying to and fro,
Rocked by all the winds that blow,
Bright with sunshine from above
Dark with shadow from below,
Beak to beak and breast to breast
In the cradle of their nest,
Lie the fledglings of our love.

**ECHO**
Love! love!

**EPIMETHEUS**
Hark! listen!  Hear how sweetly overhead
The feathered flute-players pipe their songs of love,
And echo answers, love and only love.

**CHORUS OF BIRDS**
Every flutter of the wing,
Every note of song we sing,
Every murmur, every tone,
Is of love and love alone.

**ECHO**
Love alone!

**EPIMETHEUS**
Who would not love, if loving she might be
Changed like Callisto to a star in heaven?

**PANDORA**
Ah, who would love, if loving she might be
Like Semele consumed and burnt to ashes?

**EPIMETHEUS**
Whence knowest thou these stories?

**PANDORA**

Hermes taught me;
He told me all the history of the Gods.

**CHORUS OF REEDS**
Evermore a sound shall be
In the reeds of Arcady,
Evermore a low lament
Of unrest and discontent,
As the story is retold
Of the nymph so coy and cold,
Who with frightened feet outran
The pursuing steps of Pan.

**EPIMETHEUS**
The pipe of Pan out of these reeds is made,
And when he plays upon it to the shepherds
They pity him, so mournful is the sound.
Be thou not coy and cold as Syrinx was.

**PANDORA**
Nor thou as Pan be rude and mannerless.

**PROMETHEUS** [Without
Ho! Epimetheus!

**EPIMETHEUS**
'T is my brother's voice;
A sound unwelcome and inopportune
As was the braying of Silenus' ass,
Once heard in Cybele's garden.

**PANDORA**
Let me go.
I would not be found here. I would not see him.

(She escapes among the trees.)

**CHORUS OF DRYADES**
Haste and hide thee,
Ere too late,
In these thickets intricate;
Lest Prometheus
See and chide thee,
Lest some hurt
Or harm betide thee,
Haste and hide thee!

**PROMETHEUS** [Entering.]

Who was it fled from here?  I saw a shape
Flitting among the trees.

**EPIMETHEUS**
It was Pandora.

**PROMETHEUS**
O Epimetheus!  Is it then in vain
That I have warned thee?  Let me now implore.
Thou harborest in thy house a dangerous guest.

**EPIMETHEUS**
Whom the Gods love they honor with such guests.

**PROMETHEUS**
Whom the Gods would destroy they first make mad.

**EPIMETHEUS**
Shall I refuse the gifts they send to me?

**PROMETHEUS**
Reject all gifts that come from higher powers.

**EPIMETHEUS**
Such gifts as this are not to be rejected.

**PROMETHEUS**
Make not thyself the slave of any woman.

**EPIMETHEUS**
Make not thyself the judge of any man.

**PROMETHEUS**
I judge thee not; for thou art more than man;
Thou art descended from Titanic race,
And hast a Titan's strength, and faculties
That make thee godlike; and thou sittest here
Like Heracles spinning Omphale's flax,
And beaten with her sandals.

**EPIMETHEUS**
O my brother!
Thou drivest me to madness with thy taunts.

**PROMETHEUS**
And me thou drivest to madness with thy follies.
Come with me to my tower on Caucasus:
See there my forges in the roaring caverns,

Beneficent to man, and taste the joy
That springs from labor.  Read with me the stars,
And learn the virtues that lie hidden in plants,
And all things that are useful.

**EPIMETHEU5**
O my brother!
I am not as thou art.  Thou dost inherit
Our father's strength, and I our mother's weakness:
The softness of the Oceanides,
The yielding nature that cannot resist.

**PROMETHEUS**
Because thou wilt not.

**EPIMETHEUS**
Nay; because I cannot.

**PROMETHEUS**
Assert thyself; rise up to thy full height;
Shake from thy soul these dreams effeminate,
These passions born of indolence and ease.
Resolve, and thou art free.  But breathe the air
Of mountains, and their unapproachable summits
Will lift thee to the level of themselves.

**EPIMETHEUS**
The roar of forests and of waterfalls,
The rushing of a mighty wind, with loud
And undistinguishable voices calling,
Are in my ear!

**PROMETHEUS**
O, listen and obey.

**EPIMETHEUS**
Thou leadest me as a child, I follow thee.

(They go out.)

**CHORUS OF OREADES**
Centuries old are the mountains;
Their foreheads wrinkled and rifted
Helios crowns by day,
Pallid Selene by night;
From their bosoms uptossed
The snows are driven and drifted,
Like Tithonus' beard

Streaming dishevelled and white.

Thunder and tempest of wind
Their trumpets blow in the vastness;
Phantoms of mist and rain,
Cloud and the shadow of cloud,
Pass and repass by the gates
Of their inaccessible fastness;
Ever unmoved they stand,
Solemn, eternal, and proud,

**VOICES OF THE WATERS**
Flooded by rain and snow
In their inexhaustible sources,
Swollen by affluent streams
Hurrying onward and hurled
Headlong over the crags,
The impetuous water-courses,
Rush and roar and plunge
Down to the nethermost world.

Say, have the solid rocks
Into streams of silver been melted,
Flowing over the plains,
Spreading to lakes in the fields?
Or have the mountains, the giants,
The ice-helmed, the forest-belted,
Scattered their arms abroad;
Flung in the meadows their shields?

**VOICES OF THE WINDS**
High on their turreted cliffs
That bolts of thunder have shattered,
Storm-winds muster and blow
Trumpets of terrible breath;
Then from the gateways rush,
And before them routed and scattered
Sullen the cloud-rack flies,
Pale with the pallor of death.

Onward the hurricane rides,
And flee for shelter the shepherds;
White are the frightened leaves,
Harvests with terror are white;
Panic seizes the herds,
And even the lions and leopards,
Prowling no longer for prey,
Crouch in their caverns with fright.

**VOICES OF THE FOREST**
Guarding the mountains around
Majestic the forests are standing,
Bright are their crested helms,
Dark is their armor of leaves;
Filled with the breath of freedom
Each bosom subsiding, expanding,
Now like the ocean sinks,
Now like the ocean upheaves.

Planted firm on the rock,
With foreheads stern and defiant,
Loud they shout to the winds,
Loud to the tempest they call;
Naught but Olympian thunders,
That blasted Titan and Giant,
Them can uproot and o'erthrow,
Shaking the earth with their fall.

**CHORUS OF OREADES**
These are the Voices Three
Of winds and forests and fountains,
Voices of earth and of air,
Murmur and rushing of streams,
Making together one sound,
The mysterious voice of the mountains,
Waking the sluggard that sleeps,
Waking the dreamer of dreams.

These are the Voices Three,
That speak of endless endeavor,
Speak of endurance and strength,
Triumph and fulness of fame,
Sounding about the world,
An inspiration forever,
Stirring the hearts of men,
Shaping their end and their aim.


VII

THE HOUSE OF EPIMETHEUS

**PANDORA**
Left to myself I wander as I will,
And as my fancy leads me, through this house,

Nor could I ask a dwelling more complete
Were I indeed the Goddess that he deems me.
No mansion of Olympus, framed to be
The habitation of the Immortal Gods,
Can be more beautiful.  And this is mine
And more than this, the love wherewith he crowns me.
As if impelled by powers invisible
And irresistible, my steps return
Unto this spacious hall.  All corridors
And passages lead hither, and all doors
But open into it.  Yon mysterious chest
Attracts and fascinates me.  Would I knew
What there lies hidden!  But the oracle
Forbids.  Ah me!  The secret then is safe.
So would it be if it were in my keeping.
A crowd of shadowy faces from the mirrors
That line these walls are watching me.  I dare not
Lift up the lid.  A hundred times the act
Would be repeated, and the secret seen
By twice a hundred incorporeal eyes.

(She walks to the other side of the hall.)

My feet are weary, wandering to and fro,
My eyes with seeing and my heart with waiting.
I will lie here and rest till he returns,
Who is my dawn, my day, my Helios.

(Throws herself upon a couch, and falls asleep.)

**ZEPHYRUS**
Come from thy caverns dark and deep.
O son of Erebus and Night;
All sense of hearing and of sight
Enfold in the serene delight
And quietude of sleep!

Set all the silent sentinels
To bar and guard the Ivory Gate,
And keep the evil dreams of fate
And falsehood and infernal hate
Imprisoned in their cells.

But open wide the Gate of Horn,
Whence, beautiful as planets, rise
The dreams of truth, with starry eyes,
And all the wondrous prophecies
And visions of the morn.

CHORUS OF DREAMS FROM THE IVORY GATE

Ye sentinels of sleep,
It is in vain ye keep
Your drowsy watch before the Ivory Gate;
Though closed the portal seems,
The airy feet of dreams
Ye cannot thus in walls incarcerate.

We phantoms are and dreams
Born by Tartarean streams,
As ministers of the infernal powers;
O son of Erebus
And Night, behold! we thus
Elude your watchful warders on the towers!

From gloomy Tartarus
The Fates have summoned us
To whisper in her ear, who lies asleep,
A tale to fan the fire
Of her insane desire
To know a secret that the Gods would keep.

This passion, in their ire,
The Gods themselves inspire,
To vex mankind with evils manifold,
So that disease and pain
O'er the whole earth may reign,
And nevermore return the Age of Gold.

**PANDORA** [Wwaking]
A voice said in my sleep: "Do not delay:
Do not delay; the golden moments fly!
The oracle hath forbidden; yet not thee
Doth it forbid, but Epimetheus only!"
I am alone.  These faces in the mirrors
Are but the shadows and phantoms of myself;
They cannot help nor hinder.  No one sees me,
Save the all-seeing Gods, who, knowing good
And knowing evil, have created me
Such as I am, and filled me with desire
Of knowing good and evil like themselves.

(She approaches the chest.)

I hesitate no longer.  Weal or woe,
Or life or death, the moment shall decide.

[She lifts the lid.  A dense mist rises from the chest, and fills the room.  **PANDORA** falls senseless on the floor.  Storm without.]


CHORUS OF DREAMS FROM THE GATE OF HORN

Yes, the moment shall decide!
It already hath decided;
And the secret once confided
To the keeping of the Titan
Now is flying far and wide,
Whispered, told on every side,
To disquiet and to frighten.

Fever of the heart and brain,
Sorrow, pestilence, and pain,
Moans of anguish, maniac laughter,
All the evils that hereafter
Shall afflict and vex mankind,
All into the air have risen
From the chambers of their prison;
Only Hope remains behind.


VIII

IN THE GARDEN

**EPIMETHEUS**
The storm is past, but it hath left behind it
Ruin and desolation.  All the walks
Are strewn with shattered boughs; the birds are silent;
The flowers, downtrodden by the wind, lie dead;
The swollen rivulet sobs with secret pain,
The melancholy reeds whisper together
As if some dreadful deed had been committed
They dare not name, and all the air is heavy
With an unspoken sorrow!  Premonitions,
Foreshadowings of some terrible disaster
Oppress my heart.  Ye Gods, avert the omen!

**PANDORA** [Coming from the house]
O Epimetheus, I no longer dare

To lift mine eyes to thine, nor hear thy voice,
Being no longer worthy of thy love.

**EPIMETHEUS**
What hast thou done?

**PANDORA**
Forgive me not, but kill me.

**EPIMETHEUS**
What hast thou done?

**PANDORA**
I pray for death, not pardon.

**EPIMETHEUS**
What hast thou done?

**PANDORA**
I dare not speak of it.

**EPIMETHEUS**
Thy pallor and thy silence terrify me!

**PANDORA**
I have brought wrath and ruin on thy house!
My heart hath braved the oracle that guarded
The fatal secret from us, and my hand
Lifted the lid of the mysterious chest!

**EPIMETHEUS**
Then all is lost!  I am indeed undone.

**PANDORA**
I pray for punishment, and not for pardon.

**EPIMETHEUS**
Mine is the fault not thine.  On me shall fall
The vengeance of the Gods, for I betrayed
Their secret when, in evil hour, I said
It was a secret; when, in evil hour,
I left thee here alone to this temptation.
Why did I leave thee?

**PANDORA**
Why didst thou return?
Eternal absence would have been to me
The greatest punishment.  To be left alone

And face to face with my own crime, had been
Just retribution.  Upon me, ye Gods,
Let all your vengeance fall!

**EPIMETHEUS**
On thee and me.
I do not love thee less for what is done,
And cannot be undone.  Thy very weakness
Hath brought thee nearer to me, and henceforth
My love will have a sense of pity in it,
Making it less a worship than before.

**PANDORA**
Pity me not; pity is degradation.
Love me and kill me.

**EPIMETHEUS**
Beautiful Pandora!
Thou art a Goddess still!

**PANDORA**
I am a woman;
And the insurgent demon in my nature,
That made me brave the oracle, revolts
At pity and compassion.  Let me die;
What else remains for me?

**EPIMETHEUS**
Youth, hope, and love:
To build a new life on a ruined life,
To make the future fairer than the past,
And make the past appear a troubled dream.
Even now in passing through the garden walks
Upon the ground I saw a fallen nest
Ruined and full of rain; and over me
Beheld the uncomplaining birds already
Busy in building a new habitation.

**PANDORA**
Auspicious omen!

**EPIMETHEUS**
May the Eumenides
Put out their torches and behold us not,
And fling away their whips of scorpions
And touch us not.

**PANDORA**

Me let them punish.
Only through punishment of our evil deeds,
Only through suffering, are we reconciled
To the immortal Gods and to ourselves.


CHORUS OF THE EUMENIDES

Never shall souls like these
Escape the Eumenides,
The daughters dark of Acheron and Night!
Unquenched our torches glare,
Our scourges in the air
Send forth prophetic sounds before they smite.

Never by lapse of time
The soul defaced by crime
Into its former self returns again;
For every guilty deed
Holds in itself the seed
Of retribution and undying pain.

Never shall be the loss
Restored, till Helios
Hath purified them with his heavenly fires;
Then what was lost is won,
And the new life begun,
Kindled with nobler passions and desires.


Henry Wadsworth Longfellow – A Short Biography

Henry Wadsworth Longfellow was born on February 27th, 1807 in Portland, Maine (then part of Massachusetts) to Stephen Longfellow and Zilpah (nee Wadsworth) Longfellow. His father was a lawyer, and his maternal grandfather, Peleg Wadsworth, was a general in the American Revolutionary War and a Member of Congress.

It was a large family. Longfellow was the second of eight children; his siblings were Stephen (1805), Elizabeth (1808), Anne (1810), Alexander (1814), Mary (1816), Ellen (1818) and Samuel (1819).

Longfellow attended a dame school at the age of three and by age six was enrolled at the private Portland Academy. He was very studious and quickly became fluent in Latin. His mother encouraged his love of reading and learning and introduced him to many literary classics.

He published his first poem, a patriotic four-stanza affair entitled "The Battle of Lovell's Pond", in the Portland Gazette on November 17, 1820. He remained at the Portland Academy until he was fourteen. As a child, he spent much of his summers at his grandfather Peleg's farm in the nearby town of Hiram.

In the fall of 1822, the 15-year-old Longfellow enrolled at Bowdoin College in Brunswick, Maine. His grandfather was a founder of the college and his father a trustee. Here he met and befriended Nathaniel Hawthorne. Longfellow was already thinking of a career in literature. In his senior year he wrote to his father: "I will not disguise it in the least... the fact is, I most eagerly aspire after future eminence in literature, my whole soul burns most ardently after it, and every earthly thought centers in it... I am almost confident in believing, that if I can ever rise in the world it must be by the exercise of my talents in the wide field of literature."

Poetry was the writing form he felt most at ease with and he offered poems to many newspapers and magazines. Between January 1824 and graduation in 1825, he had almost 40 poems published, over half of which were in the short-lived Boston periodical The United States Literary Gazette.

When Longfellow graduated, he was ranked a pleasing fourth in the class, and had been elected to Phi Beta Kappa. He was quickly offered the post of professor of modern languages at his alma mater.

Accounts suggest that part of the requirement of acceptance was to tour Europe to become more immersed in both languages and cultures. Longfellow began his tour of Europe in May 1826 aboard the ship Cadmus. His travels in Europe would last three years and cost his father the princely sum of $2,604.24. He visited France, Spain, Italy, Germany and England before returning to the United States in mid-August 1829.

His stock of languages now included French, Spanish, Portuguese, and German, and impressively, mostly without any formal instruction.

On August 27th, 1829, he wrote to the president of Bowdoin that he was turning down the professorship because he considered the $600 salary "disproportionate to the duties required". The trustees countered by raising the salary to $800 and an additional $100 to serve as the college's librarian, a post which required only one hour's attention a day.

On September 14th, 1831, Longfellow married Mary Storer Potter, a childhood friend from Portland. The couple settled in Brunswick. Longfellow now published several non-fiction and fiction prose pieces inspired by his friend Washington Irving, whom he had met in Madrid during his travels, these included "The Indian Summer" and "The Bald Eagle" in 1833.

During his years teaching at the college, he translated textbooks in French, Italian and Spanish; his first published book was in 1833, a translation of the poetry of the medieval Spanish poet Jorge Manrique. A travel book, Outre-Mer: A Pilgrimage Beyond the Sea, was first published in serial form before a book edition in 1835.

In December 1834, Longfellow received a letter from Josiah Quincy III, president of Harvard College, offering him the Smith Professorship of Modern Languages with the condition that he first spend a year or so abroad. The Longfellow's set off for Europe. He would now be able to add German, Dutch, Danish, Swedish, Finnish, and Icelandic to his repertoire of languages.

During the trip they discovered that Mary was pregnant. Sadly, in October 1835, she miscarried some six months into the pregnancy. Then followed several weeks of illness and at the age of 22 on November 29th, 1835 she died. Longfellow had her body embalmed, placed in a lead coffin itself inside an oak coffin which was then shipped to Mount Auburn Cemetery near Boston. He wrote movingly "One thought occupies me night and day... She is dead—She is dead! All day I am weary and sad".

Back in the United States, Longfellow took up the professorship at Harvard. He was required to live in Cambridge, close to the campus and rented rooms at the Craigie House in the spring of 1837. The home, built in 1759, had once been the headquarters of George Washington during the Siege of Boston.

Longfellow now felt able to publish again, starting with the collection Voices of the Night in 1839. It was mainly comprised of translations together with nine original poems and seven poems written back in his teenage years.

His romantic interests also began to surface again. He had begun to court Frances 'Fanny' Appleton, daughter of the Boston industrialist Nathan Appleton. At first, the independent-minded Appleton was not interested in marriage but Longfellow was determined. In July 1839, he wrote to a friend: "Victory hangs doubtful. The lady says she will not! I say she shall! It is not pride, but the madness of passion".

In late 1839, Longfellow published Hyperion, a book in prose inspired by his trips abroad and his still un-successful courtship of Fanny Appleton. Amidst this, Longfellow fell into "periods of neurotic depression with moments of panic" and required a six-month leave of absence from Harvard to attend a health spa in the former Marienberg Benedictine Convent at Boppard in Germany.

Ballads and Other Poems was published in 1841 and included "The Village Blacksmith" and "The Wreck of the Hesperus". His reputation as a poet, and a commercial one at that, was set.

Longfellow published a play in 1842, The Spanish Student, based on his memories from his time in Spain in the 1820s. A small collection, Poems on Slavery, was also published in 1842. This was Longfellow's first public support of abolitionism. However, as Longfellow himself said, the poems were "so mild that even a Slaveholder might read them without losing his appetite for breakfast". The New England Anti-Slavery Association, however, was satisfied enough with the intent of the collection to reprint it for their own distribution.

On May 10th, 1843, after seven years in pursuit, Longfellow received a letter from Fanny Appleton agreeing to marry him. He was elated and immediately walked 90 minutes to meet her at her house.

Nathan Appleton bought the Craigie House as a wedding present to the pair. Longfellow lived there for the rest of his life. His love for Fanny is evident from Longfellow's only love poem, the sonnet "The Evening Star", written in October 1845:

"O my beloved, my sweet Hesperus!
My morning and my evening star of love!"

He once attended a ball without her and said, "The lights seemed dimmer, the music sadder, the flowers fewer, and the women less fair."

Longfellow and Fanny had six children: Charles Appleton (1844), Ernest Wadsworth (1845), Fanny (1847, who died in infancy), Alice Mary (1850), Edith (1853), and Anne Allegra (1855).

Aware of his growing stature and his ability to influence others he also encouraged and supported many other translators. In 1845, he published The Poets and Poetry of Europe, a large 800-page compendium of translated works by other writers. Longfellow intended the anthology "to bring together, into a compact and convenient form, as large an amount as possible of those English translations which are scattered through many volumes, and are not accessible to the general reader".

On November 1st, 1847, the epic poem Evangeline was published.

Longfellow's literary income was now becoming quite substantial: in 1840, he had made $219 but by 1850 it had grown to a very promising $1,900.

On June 14th, 1853, Longfellow held a farewell dinner party at his Cambridge home for his great friend Nathaniel Hawthorne, who was preparing to move overseas.

In 1854, Longfellow retired from Harvard, devoting himself entirely to writing. He would be awarded an honorary doctorate of laws from Harvard in 1859.

The Song of Haiwatha, his epic poem, and perhaps his best known and enjoyed work was published in 1855.

On a hot July 9th day, 1861, Fanny was putting several locks of her children's hair into an envelope and making attempts to seal it with hot sealing wax while Longfellow took a nap. The circumstances of what happened next vary but the actuality is that Fanny's dress caught fire. Her screams awakened Longfellow who rushed to help her and threw a rug over her and stifled the flames with his own body as best he could, but Fanny was already horrifically burned.

A doctor was called and Fanny was taken to her room to recover. She was in and out of consciousness throughout the night and was also administered ether. The next morning, July 10th, 1861, she died shortly after 10 o'clock after asking for a cup of coffee.

Longfellow, in his effort to save her had also been badly burned and was unable to attend her funeral. His facial injuries required he stopped shaving. The ensuing beard now became the quintessential look that everyone remembers from pictures.

Devastated, he never fully recovered and sometimes resorted to laudanum and ether to ease the pain. He worried he would go insane and begged "not to be sent to an asylum" and noted that he was "inwardly bleeding to death". In the sonnet "The Cross of Snow" (1879), which he wrote eighteen years later he wrote:

"Such is the cross I wear upon my breast
These eighteen years, through all the changing scenes
And seasons, changeless since the day she died".

Longfellow spent several years translating Dante Alighieri's epic poem, The Divine Comedy. To aid him in perfecting the translation and reviewing proofs, he invited several friends to weekly meetings every

Wednesday from 1864. This became known as the "Dante Club", and regulars included William Dean Howells, James Russell Lowell, Charles Eliot Norton and other occasional guests. The full three-volume translation was published in the spring of 1867, though Longfellow would continue to revise it. It was wildly popular and was re-printed four times in its first year.

By 1868, Longfellow's annual income was over a staggering $48,000.

Longfellow was also part of a group of Poets who became known as The Fireside Poets. The group included Longfellow, William Cullen Bryant, John Greenleaf Whittier, James Russell Lowell, and Oliver Wendell Holmes Snr. Occasionally Ralph Waldo Emerson is also placed among their number. The name "Fireside Poets" derives from poetry reading as a collective family entertainment of the times.

During the 1860s, Longfellow, still a committed abolitionist, also hoped for a coming together, a reconciliation, between the north and south after the dark days of the Civil War. When his son was wounded during the war, he wrote the poem "Christmas Bells", later the basis of the carol I Heard the Bells on Christmas Day.

In 1874, Samuel Cutler Ward helped him sell the poem "The Hanging of the Crane" to the New York Ledger for $3,000; it was the highest price ever paid for a poem. An astonishing sum. But Longfellow was worth it. His fame and audience were widespread and devoted.

Continuing in his hopes for a better and more united America he wrote in his journal in 1878: "I have only one desire; and that is for harmony, and a frank and honest understanding between North and South". Longfellow, despite his aversion to public speaking, took up an offer from Joshua Chamberlain to speak at his fiftieth reunion at Bowdoin College. Here he read the poem "Morituri Salutamus" so quietly that few could hear.

On August 22th, 1879, a female admirer who seemed to know little about his history, traveled to Longfellow's house in Cambridge and, unaware to whom she was speaking, asked Longfellow: "Is this the house where Longfellow was born?" Longfellow told her it was not. The visitor then asked if he had died here. "Not yet", he replied.

Much of Longfellow's work is recognized for its melody-like musicality. As he says, "what a writer asks of his reader is not so much to like as to listen".

Longfellow, like many others of the period, called for the development of high quality American literature. In his work, Kavanagh, a character says: "We want a national literature commensurate with our mountains and rivers... We want a national epic that shall correspond to the size of the country... We want a national drama in which scope shall be given to our gigantic ideas and to the unparalleled activity of our people... In a word, we want a national literature altogether shaggy and unshorn, that shall shake the earth, like a herd of buffaloes thundering over the prairies."

As a translator Longfellow was very impressive. His translation of Dante's The Divine Comedy became a requirement for those who wanted to be a part of high culture.

In 1874, Longfellow oversaw a 31-volume anthology called Poems of Places, collecting poems of several geographical locations; Europe, Asia, and the Arabian countries. It was a work of great educational endeavor but Emerson was disappointed and is said to have told Longfellow: "The world is expecting better things of you than this... You are wasting time that should be bestowed upon original production".

At this point in his life Longfellow could look back and see that his early collections, Voices of the Night and Ballads and Other Poems, had made him instantly popular. The New-Yorker called him "one of the very few in our time who has successfully aimed in putting poetry to its best and sweetest uses". The Southern Literary Messenger immediately put Longfellow "among the first of our American poets".

The rapidity with which American readers embraced Longfellow was unparalleled in publishing history in the United States. His popularity spread throughout Europe, his poems translated into Italian, French, German, and other languages.

Longfellow was the most popular poet of his day. As a friend once wrote to him, "no other poet was so fully recognized in his lifetime". Some of his works including "Paul Revere's Ride" and "The Song of Haiwatha" may have rewritten the facts but became essential parts of the American psyche and culture. He was so admired that on his 70th birthday in 1877 the atmosphere was that of a national holiday, with parades, speeches, and, of course, the reading of his poems.

Over the years, Longfellow's reputation came to include his personality; he was a gentle, placid, poetic soul. James Russell Lowell said, Longfellow had an "absolute sweetness, simplicity, and modesty". The reality was that Longfellow's life was much more difficult than was assumed. He suffered from neuralgia, which caused him constant pain, and poor eyesight. The difficulties of coping with the loss of two wives also took its toll.  He was very quiet, reserved, and private; in later years, he became increasingly unsocial and avoided leaving home if he could.

In March 1882, Longfellow went to bed with severe stomach pain. He endured the pain for several days with the help of opium.

Henry Wadsworth Longfellow died, surrounded by family, on Friday, March 24th, 1882. He had been suffering from peritonitis.

He is buried with both of his wives at Mount Auburn Cemetery in Cambridge, Massachusetts. At Longfellow's funeral, his friend Ralph Waldo Emerson called him "a sweet and beautiful soul".

At the time of his death, his estate was valued at $356,320.

In 1884, Longfellow became the first non-British writer for whom a sculpted bust was placed in Poet's Corner of Westminster Abbey in London; he remains the sole American poet thus represented.


Henry Wadsworth Longfellow – A Concise Bibliography

Outre-Mer: A Pilgrimage Beyond the Sea (Travelogue) (1835)
Hyperion, a Romance (1839)
The Spanish Student. A Play in Three Acts (1843)
Evangeline: A Tale of Acadie (poem) (1847)
Kavanagh (1849)

The Golden Legend (poem) (1851)
The Song of Hiawatha (poem) (1855)
The New England Tragedies (1868)
The Divine Tragedy (1871)
Christus: A Mystery (1872)
Aftermath (poem) (1873)
The Arrow and the Song (poem)

## Poetry Collections

Voices of the Night (1839)
Ballads & Other Poems (1841)
Poems on Slavery (1842)
The Belfry of Bruges & Other Poems (1845)
The Seaside and the Fireside (1850)
The Poetical Works of Henry Wadsworth Longfellow (1852)
The Courtship of Miles Standish & Other Poems (1858)
Tales of a Wayside Inn (1863)
Birds of Passage (1863)
Household Poems (1865)
Flower-de-Luce (1867)
Three Books of Song (1872)
The Masque of Pandora & Other Poems (1875)
Kéramos & Other Poems (1878)
Ultima Thule (1880)
In the Harbor (1882)
Michel Angelo: A Fragment (incomplete; published posthumously)

## Translations

Coplas de Don Jorge Manrique (Translation from Spanish) (1833)
Dante's Divine Comedy (Translation) (1867)

## Anthologies

Poets and Poetry of Europe (Translations) (1845)
The Waif (1845)
Poems of Places (1874)

www.ingramcontent.com/pod-product-compliance
Lightning Source LLC
Chambersburg PA
CBHW060106050426
42448CB00011B/2640